Overtide

Overtide

By Tricia Jones

Published by Tricia Jones

Copyright © 2008
Tricia Jones

The right of Tricia Jones to be identified as the author of this
work has been asserted by her in accordance with the Copyright,
Designs and Patents Act 1988.

ISBN: 978-0-9545762-8-8

Printed and bound in Great Britain by:
Limited Editions, Remus House, Coltsfoot Drive
Woodston, Peterborough PE2 9JX

Previous Publications 'Overtide' by Tricia Jones

Acknowledgement

With a love like this deep under the ocean.

Contents

Part One – Empty Bottle

Part Two – Silly half Hour

Part Three – Love Doesn't Make Any Sense

Part Four – Melted Icicles

Part One –Empty Bottle

1. Age

As the seconds
Ticked by
She turned into stone
With each second
Was a hundred years
And she could not hang
Onto youth
A withered leaf
In an ice-age
Where love bloomed
His innocence
Lost her
And he was on his own
With teardrops
In heaven.

2. Tea-tasting

A cup of tea, an afternoon meal
Or light refreshment at which
Tea is generally served, a cooked meal
Take in the early evening, high tea
To look with a fixed gaze, to glare
To be insistently or obtrusively conspicuous
To be all too obvious
A quick motion of the eye
The time occupied by a wink
An instant, the scintillation of the fixed stars
Eyes meet over the table.

3. River

Seagulls roam and fly with me
Fluttering to keep height and balance
Like in a thermal gliding into space
Dropping, fluttering to keep height
Diving in a crash depth to land on
A tree trunk, like insects in a rain forest
Landing safe from home.

4. Goodnight

The wind, the rain, the flowers
In a rocking chair your shape
Glued to the wood on cushions of heather
Singing a lullaby to the sounds of the waves.

5. Empty Bottle

Indian head band on round campfire
Sparks with sea-spray, I love you
Wind whistling, chill shivering, but boiling
Burnt out from dancing hand in hand, grit in face
Sand storm seaweed hanging from hair, dancing
On the sands dead of night, in paradise.

6. Spirit

The spirit of love, never disappears, with fallen leaves.

7. When

We will swim beneath the waves, at the turning of the tide,
Washed in the spray, of a thousand drops of rain.

8. Silence

Yellow furnace, a dangerous position,
Bubbling, hot spring, face of the sun.

9. Fading

On lily pond, shadows wave, with fans in the dark, petals
echo in the water.
Lovers kiss, in time forgotten, rain circles on water, to
spit or throw out moisture, in scattered drops. On muddy
pond, lullaby reeds, talking bush, walking trees. Mere
noise, without meaning or sense, or distinguished from
sense, a mental impression, weeds listening, sprouting
flowers, runaway stilts growing to the sky.
Holding hands for eternity, in the depths of the night.

10. Thunder

With breath the sun's rays,
Blow dry with ringlets,
And clips,
Combed with twigs.

11. Them

In a garden on a bench with arms around each other,
To smoke with puffs, a pipe. To say something, to begin
to speak.
The gases, vapours and fine particles that are emitted by
burning material.
A cloud or column of fumes, something that may be
smoked.
Smoke a cigarette just sitting together, to exhale or
emit smoke.
Vapour, dust to send smoke in the wrong direction.
A break
For a smoke during the working day, now a rest, a tea
break.
Soaking in the sun and the rain together for eternity.

12. Thoughts

Current strong, sun glowing on light spot water, to
advance in rank fortune.
Posy of wild flowers, guard of honour with twigs an
expensive stylish and luxurious establishment. Raft pull
across, green, black and grey, a poll which a person sits
astride, to cross a river, to fasten with rivets. Blue
knuckled sea, wading offshore.

13. One Minuet

A dish of thick coated stew, with chicken and carrots,
onions and other vegetables and cheese. A shoe moulded
from untanned hide, worn with the hair to the outside.
Tatters, rags, a drinking cry.
Knuckles red, numb cold hands.
Shallow dark water, tired but happy, reeds, straw.

14. Lone

A type of Italian folksong with eight-line stanzas, or a
piece of music written in the same style, audaciously.
Bordering on the unseemly, a sardonic grin or drawing
back of the corners of the mouth by spasm of the
muscles.
High in stature as in six feet tall, the tendency or
desire to cut any successful or prominent person down to
size. A place where friends meet and live, floating
circles, lime and orange withered edge, kissing under the
shade of an old oak tree, with white flower, water lilies.

15. Flight

Dove of peace, reassurance,
Flying forever.

16. Waiting

Waving shadows on brick as night falls
Sunset fading, dandelion seeds floating past
Blowing aimlessly, rooftops black, tall buildings
Stretching way up to the sky, full of stars,
To guide the way to your heart.

17. Hooked

A wicker basket, a coop,
A person who carries fish inland to sell,
Face with glee, toothy smile,
With the sun, wind and rain as your guide.

18. Now

Rough and raw, entwined
Arms clasped in togetherness
Until the end of time.

19. One

Roar of engine, takes off along the water,
Or nearly all, the orchestra or choir,
Brown sun-tanned arm, wet sandals.
Get dressed up to impress, stylish, elegant
Stretch of broken water, disturbed state of the sea,
Loose broken stones used to form a foundation,
On soft ground or underwater, a little wave,
A process in which a trend or situation
Spread outward from its initial location
To affect areas distant from it,
An adulatory ridging produced in sediments,
By waves currents and wind,
Often produced in sedimentary rocks.
Able or inclined to laugh, of laughter,
Ludicrous.
Ready for harvest, arrived at perfection,
Fit for use.
To answer with a riposte.
Dry mud cakes on knees, snow bubbles wading,
A necklace of diamonds or other precious stones
in several strings.
Who returned home after having slept
In the mountains for twenty years.

20. Peace

The sea, the sand, the waves, sitting on the pebbles
And feeling the water glistening in the shells
The sunlight, the breeze, blowing your hair
Feel the sun beating down, a seagull cry,
In the whistling of the wind.

21. Fingertips

Tears from heaven in a worn-out face, head-massage,
tired.
Comforting, healing, happy, content, eyes closed,
Showing the years, hands clasped together, in a oneness,
Eyes glistening, grey hair like the sun, sparkling.

22. Crystal

You'll be in a pool of ice
And I'll sing you to sleep
Lullaby in heaven
Eagles wings in the stars.

23. Together

Ice in my heart, zero temperature,
Fast rain, cold waves of silk.
Round dents in the water, ebbing towards you, engulfing,
Singing, fluttering to your heart.

24. Lullaby

Swept by
The tide
Two bodies
Who weren't
Meant to be
Together

25. Glaze

Not understanding each other but looking into
His eyes like tornadoes, watery, sparkling, in the dust of
the day. Moonshine, sunset, a shadow of uncut diamonds.
His long lingering stare, glazed with thoughts, forbidden.

26. Winter Coat

I just want to go to sleep in his arms
A thousand tornadoes in spring.
A cold breeze, shiver in the space, howling
Empty streets
Wrapped in warmth.

27. Surfing

Into the unknown, clasped hands.
Hold tight here we go.
Knee plaster all in hand.
Laughter, fun.
Spitting water.
Upon the land.
Roaring ocean plays.
Grazed knee.
With sand pebbles.

28. Iceblink

A reflection from fields of snow.
Like iceblink.
Snow falling off branches.
Icicles on line.
Glowing in the sun.
Leaves dripping.
Crispy white.

29. Guitar Wind

The wind is like a wheel going around, thunder crashes
on the windows, the rain-sweep of storm battles outside
like a steam engine.
Water pours and shakes wind in turmoil. The ticking of
the clock sounds at 3am, the house is edged in darkness
as sleep overtakes.
Galloping horses, knights in shining armour battle with
the torment.
A crow outside made a conversation with an early
morning alarm clock.
Clusters of birds line the trees singing as breakfast dawns
with porridge.

30. The Hug

I drag you along the concrete stone.
With a fag in mouth, foaming with scented shampoo
As our bodies touch the rough paving stone
Crying out in pain, foreheads touching,
Noses rubbing, kissing in lover's embrace.

31. Sight

I love you from distance apart.
When the wind blows and icicles tear
At the turning of the tide.

32. Moon-Flower

Waters of life, tingling, thrilling, raging seas over rocks,
in mid-streams, in currents, under the sea where mer'folk
reign,
Predominance, predominating influence, kingdom, realm,
domain.
Blowing bubbles and shapes dancing hand in hand, of
life, seaweed forms, stormy or furious tides, madness,
overpowering passion of any kind,
anger, inspired frenzy.
Shade of the moon.
Racing over the shingles.
For eternity.

33. Climb A Mountain

He could control with the eyes, and the guitar played
from the soul.
Command armies, keep an eye on a room, keep
conversation going.
And the sky opened up, and keep his way with attention.
With a flicker of an eye lash, a strict look, all he wanted
was company.
And attention, a sort of telepathy and strong music.
Head of the pack, happy in his way and a leader.

34. Danger

The moon glistens
with the early morning dew.

35. Grin

Love lit up the sky,
You blew deep foggy breath,
Of cool fire,
As you showed your teeth,
In your warm smile.

36. Tent Caterpillar

A portable shelter of canvas or other cloth, driven into the
ground to fasten a tent, sausage and beans burnt with
smoke. A bitter-tasting, bright red Italian aperitif
flavoured with herbs. An act of telling a narrative story, a
false story, a mere story, things told idly or to get others
in trouble. A solid essential oil derived from the camphor
laurel, having an aromatic smell and bitter taste used as a
liniment in medicine and as an insect repellent. The
continuous succession of thoughts, emotions and
feelings, both vague and well-defined that forms an
individual's conscious experience. A party or group
supporting a certain set of beliefs or doctrine. To pack up
tents, equipment etc and leave a camp.
Lying beneath the clouds, specks of rain like tear-dust, in
the early morning dew.

37. Outside

Vapour, mist, rising above the ground, off the freezing
pavement.
You are in my thoughts and will never disappear,
blackened street,
Sharp frost, lighted candle street lamp, shining in glory,
The rain pours splattering on the windows, as the edge of
night,
Is like cut glass fading as dawn approaches.

38. Blade

I was going to
Embrace you
On the thinnest grass,
But stopped on a bed
Of roses.

39. Still

The rooftops shade of lilac in the calm of the forest, the
ferns blow, spiky,
waving from side to side, navy deep blue sky darkened at
night.
Peace with a lamp post shine, glow in the dark, showing
purple pathway.
Through deep green grass, silence, stillness, but for the
thumping of your heart.

40. He

An image, of long ago, protecting, strong.
Towering above, read my mind and act in sharing.
Hidden thoughts, in a secret garden,
only to be scattered in the wind.

41. Tough

The sun bright on the crisp dew grass,
Patches and clumps saturated wooden bench,
empty. Crystals in the eye beaming upon the face
in the unknown window, old broken pane. In a
tower of ice, where the waves cannot foam.
But the forest is calling, but where peace reigns.
Only for a snatched moment before a shower of hail.

42. Youth

The sun shown down, coaxing, restoring, gentle winds.
In all its beauty, yellow, brown, red, yet crumbles in
hand
A withered leaf.
Ice came down, hanging in spears.

43. One

Worn slippers on and a hot drink, slink into slumber land.
Fade away into nothingness, but extreme pleasure
of tides as one with a lullaby at sea.

44. Jogging

Wind whipping hair.
His studded boots.
On sandy beach.
Grains in mouth.
With excitement.
Heavy metal.
Welcoming fate with a twist.

45. Mist

As the waves argue.
Purple sky, in the whistling of the wind.
Ejected by fire. Lust, greed, want
For a normal life.

46. Thin Air

Full of heavy water.
Spots of biting rain.
Gone in the crowd.
I love you as you are.
Face with cheek.
Taunting me.

47. Lost

To make music.
As the waves thunder.
Full of melody, pleasant to listen to.
Time within which past things,
Can be remembered.
Things worth remembering.
The act or art of writing memoirs.
A craze for music.
Song and madness.

48. Here

Stay here and relax in the cool of the evening
After a hot day of chalk and cheese
To rest in an easy chair, legs up, drinking
a hot cup of tea. Steam on glasses, hands melting the ice,
Boiling tongue, smooth over lips, as tiredness takes over.

49. Ladder

Climbing to the stars.
You put me on a rainbow.
Coloured twinkled in your eyes.

50. Forever

It's a nippy frosty night, warm inside, hot as toast,
as the wind whistles outside.

51. Companion-Start

Love is like rain, attachment from mutual esteem,
Friendly assistance, gentle breeze, he is pure, delightful.
Loving, laughter, kiss, tease, tender, passion.
A close companion, an intimate associate or friend.
A fellow shoulder, a mate,
Apart numbness, till it hurts.

52. Twelve O'clock

In your arms I lie in wonderland, listening to your breathing.
Pulse racing, central heating switched on, blackness,
stillness.
Holding hands, your beating of your heart.
Ticking of the clock in endless space and peace.
Home at last, warmth, soft skin, icy chill.
Wind beating outside.
In utter loneliness.

53. Fireguard

Slight chill, warmth from fire.
Breath of cold air, close window.
Washing steam clothes, a very crisp dry.
Glow amongst coals.

54. Roar

While the wind roars,
And the rain spits.
Fire-lights glows.

55. Chill

I just like being with you.
When the north winds blow.
Until icicles,
Appear on the window ledge.

56. Butterfly

Your face, a reflection in the pebbles, haunting.
Your very existence, bubbles.
Under the water.
Blowing kisses of death.

57. Afternoon

So content to hear you sing.
Reading the Sunday newspaper.
So absorbed with the sports page.
Keeping up with current events.
Sipping tea, rustling paper.
Loosely, ink print on hands.
Tired, but happy.

58. Gloves

Black ice on concrete, a place for the foot to rest on, a
secure and stable one,
A sock for keeping the feet warm.

59. Kiss

Your kiss is not forgotten, your wincing smile,
Of forbidden fruit, your ginger beard,
And uncombed hair, a fatal attraction,
And time will never run out.

60. Wrapper

Grey and yellow clouds sprinting across the sky,
the wind blows icy.
In corners of eyes, freezing tears, runny nose,
hair in mouth.
Spiky without their coats the bare trees frown, yellow and
silver beech tree, ancient creaking, showing its years,
embedded in the grass, propped up by a stick.
Dewdrops sparkling, spider's web gleaming on twigs,
pink and brown like Christmas tree lights and waving in
the wind. Puffing cheeks, blowing with the cold,
standing there, two tortured souls in the wind.
Crystals of snow blew down lattice jewels forming a
white, wrap-over cloak,
To dress warmly. To fold something round something, to
enfold, clothe or swathe,
To become warm or ardent, to begin to enjoy, approve of,
feel enthusiastic about or fond of.
A shawl or stole for the shoulders, an outdoor garment.
Wind breaker against the cold.

61. Read

Sometimes I can't do what people want me to do
Like go to the moon and back.

62. Frozen

The guitar plays as flakes fall, melody against the
coal fire,
Depth or brilliance of colour, a tint or shade, general
effect of colours.
Flames orange, red and blue, singing from the soul,
deep tones.
The character of a sound, vocal inflection, rise or fall
in pitch, as expressing feeling, mood.
Used as a way of distinguishing words. Damp rot
in wood,
Crackling, glowing, heat, warmth, crisp heavy snow,
Weaving its blanket.

63. Wind

Us tied,
Together,
With seaweed,
Mangled,
On a,
Shore.

64. Goodnight

I went to the moon and watch diamonds sparkle
But I could not wear one on my ring from you
Because you no longer needed me, except in paradise.

65. Choice

Throwing dust of Christmas snow on frozen lake.
Misty chilling, wrapping up warm.

66. Beard

Your beard,
Abundant in warm sea,
A small musical instrument,
Encasing metallic reeds,
Played by the mouth,
Burnt amber,
Frosty twigs,
Silver-grey,
To form silently by moving the lips,
Frog's lobes with eye of the toad blinking,
With a glow of winter warmth,
Of, from, like or lighted, coloured,
Or warmed by the sun.

67. Pool

Snow cut off the wilderness, and made it glisten,
Bird prints, brought it home, in parts through, to the
slush, in puddles of water,
As the sun came out, tufts of grass appeared, and the
ice cracked.

68. Crack Of Dawn

Peace in a dove, flying in a thermal,
In the crisp early morning air,
When the voices of the forest are alive.

69. Lover

The sun, the moon, and the stars are in your eyes,
Misty seas. You drove me up to the moon
Where I balanced on a star to see the glow
In your eyes like pearl diamonds.

70. Hair Cut

Hair appointment, waiting, anticipation,
A brush for the hair or the style in which this is done,
Looking, watching, as hair glides past onto the floor,
Someone whose occupation is the cutting, colouring,
A particular way of snipping and arranging the hair,
Looking in the mirror, reflection,
A hinged clasp, often decorative, worn in the hair,
The neat appearance, to keep up an outward show,
One that belies, or is intended to appear in person,
If only briefly.

71. Tall

You mean more to me, your scraggy hair,
Sodden face, 6ft 2ins tall. Bruised eyebrows,
Lips like fire, that make the twigs dance
In a duet to the wind.

72. Midnight

Dancing in the spray with rain-sand people,
in the dead of night with a starlit sky,
Shadows disappearing in front of the moon,
Rainbow clouds kissing shadows.

73. Silver-glance

Your face I see, calm, untouched,
unruffled, calm, brightness.
Serenity, serene sky or sea,
an image, a form I could never forget,
Pure air, everything as it should be,
all right, whiskers, a smile,
To catch a glimpse of, to direct glancingly.
Darting of the eye, a momentary look,
spoken kindly, given to speaking kindly,
Substitute for please, to burn or shine faintly.
Feeble rays of light, to eye with intense,
an inkling, faint perception,
to act according to one's nature.
To direct one's eyes
and attention.

74. Slide Guitar

To slip or glide, to pass along, over, down, smoothly,
over ice
or other slippery surface. To take its own course, white
scented sea,
Of the colour usual in leaves, growing, vigorous,
flourishing, new.
Splashing upon rocks green algae or seaweeds,
sheltering from fine specks,
brimming with, ready to shed, or shedding.
Of the face or cheeks, streaked with tracks, left by tears.
As the guitar plays, the waves whisper.

75. Evening-Light

Black metal fireguard dressing the fireplace,
sinking in deep settee, covered with knitted patchwork
quilts. Half-filled warm cups of tea, ornaments staring in
their home. Draw curtain, winter night, books well read
untidy on shelves. Loud rushing sound, water falls upon
window, pin pricks, draught around ankles, freezing air,
soaring flames of coal fire, hot furnace, wind blowing
down chimney, warmth from socks.
Undone trainers lying idle in front of the fireplace.

76. Tear-Smoke

A slight turning of the moon,
Or overflows from it,
As a manifestation of emotion,
Is visible at any one time,
An exuding drop,
To be face to face with,
Brimming with, ready to shed,
To cause to tremble,
Into the teeth of the wind,
A thrill of horror or fear,
I wiped your nose,
And you kissed my tears.

Part Two - Silly Half-Hour

77. Half-Moon

Moonbeam shadow, like snowdrops of the deep,
roaring ocean,
Crystals in the air, from the fathomless under a
starlit sky.

78. Howl

Where the suns meet the Earth in an orange glow
As we take the steps to paradise, the winds howl,
And the wolves cry out in loneliness.

79. Gone

The wind and the rain can never separate you
and me. We love as one and leave in despair
in the dream of hope for tomorrow.

80. Turn

Ruled by the moon,
in the great mystery of life,
In the eternity and the great beyond.

81. Oven Roast

So nice sitting together, with door open, cat outside in
garden amongst leaves.
Dinner cooking, finishing off the remains of a hot cup
of tea.
Soul-mate reading newspaper, delicious smells coming
from oven.

82. Moonbeam

I love you to bits of a jig-saw.
While I hold the key to a love over the moon.

83. Ring

When the snow glistened deep and the winds blew
With me over your shoulder you started the long track
To the stars overhead.

84. Glance

Goodbye as the wind whistled, you walked away over
the horizon
Until you were a tiny blob in the snow, but an earthquake
in my heart,
As the wind whistled tears of crystal trickled down
my cheeks
Until they turned into ice.

85. Glasses

I'd rather be watching than taking part,
But it is with great passion and need,
With a soul-mate forever.

86. You

I have never known such passion and care,
A need so great, love like a teardrop
With a big huggy bear.

87. Indian

Indian call of the wild, riding in smoke,
A screen of love.

88. Beard

Your rough face against mine,
Cuddle in a thousand yesterdays.

89. Melt

You looked at me with a frozen glare
That melted as soon as you saw my face.

90. Him

There is light in the middle of the window, in the dark,
I saw your face today and the Earth moved.

91. Blizzard

Where teardrops melt upon sore cheeks, freezing
pointed icicles,
A hard stony glare, first and only love, pierce a heart,
a rift in the clouds, stinging nettles, poured snow down.

92. Sent

While the storms of rage and water runs down your face,
kissed his tears, taste like salt from the ocean.

93. Gale

Cloud creatures of smoke, Angels of light, feathers
floating on rock,
disappearing, until we climb the narrow rocky path,
a guiding light, in a passage through the clouds.

94. Dew

Tears glisten in the sun shadows fall and become cold
and distant, standing at the edge of the tide, lovers
embrace, I love you the winds blow warm upon your
face.

95. Teardrop

Raindrops like neddles in the waters of the sky,
as the winds blow them apart,
Leaves twittering flying high, branches catching them,
evaporating into thin air.

96. Whisper

Into the hive of wrinkled dreams the voice of the forest
falls silent in broken make-believe that lie in wild
moments, forgotten deep in the thicket.
Praying for the white snow to come winter coat of
warmth.

97. Against The Tide

With thick coats of slime braided hair of fishbone,
Green necklace of seaweed, wearing crown of pearls,
with drops of rain, toughened skin,
Voice bellowing like thunder, a shiver in the wind,
pebbles echoing, bells, damp cold sand disappear with
the night.

98. Face

You saw the wave coming and ducked,
And came to the surface with a thousand star-lights.

99. Sun

Spit from the waterfall, the waves glistened in the sun
as you smiled,
Your eyes dull sea waters at being parted for so long.

100. Shadowless

Nothing as the wind blows,
Your presence left,
But your shadow remained.

101. Torch

Shining light from the deep,
You put me on a star and took me to paradise.

102. Never

Your thoughts are my thoughts, one shadow in
endless nights,
Of sleepwalking and daydreaming in time forgotten.

103. Salute

The gleam in your eye as you smudge away your tears,
With the hand that waved goodbye.

104. Volcano

I'm in seventh heaven with your love
A bond from the crust of the Earth.

105. Dark

Sparkling waters in ambush, waving come hither,
Lime climbing rocks underneath.
Trees spikey, tangerine, fighting waves,
Green mist, slime, sun going down, dusk.

106. Mirage

Dewdrops, wet spider's web, jewels, to occupy or
make busy.
Drops of honey on weeds, a master of ceremonies,
as the sun came up,
To make alterations, in with a view of improving.
Moist sand ripples on water, led him a dance,
guitar wind.

107. Torch

Dull waters, glittering, disappearing, edge of a gemstone,
A beautiful velvety leaf, variety of beryl its colour.
Feather grass hopping emerald-cut in gemstones.
Splashing cold hands in water, mud, purple thistles.

108. Answer

Tongue tied in a sea of loneliness,
In the wild untamed but soft and human.

109. Mist

Gliding stone beckoning, dull coloured skimming.
Silver flow, yellow, grey and pink sun, birds chirping.

110. Icicle Man

Icicles,
Dripping from
His beard,
Like a vacuum,
Cleaner I sucked,
For air.

111. Dense

Black shadow, evening dense, flat caps with piece
hanging down on cold ears.
Wearing camouflage jackets, laughter in tinted-blue
sunglasses, overcast light,
Disappears night beckons, running clouds of this deep
blue colour, of cobalt,
A blue pigment prepared from it.

112. Frost

In past the stars in the heavens or a raindrop in a pond.
Ice on mill-dew, a misty morning.

113. Mine

I love you distance away, a form in the darkness.
Waiting for myself and light.

114. Dream

A teardrop in your eye, birds in the sky,
Or your first kiss, an hour, a diamond in make-believe.

115. Leap Beyond

Twisted smile, pinprick to fingertips.
Call of the wild in the night.

116. Pathway

Your figure distant away, as tears glistened in the snow,
You took the path to loneliness.

117. Pebbles

The moon yawned,
Into the arms of the sun.

118. Away

Stars sparkled in your eyes, in loneliness, before the
tide took you away,
Warm seas brought back your deep glow.

119. Out

The world at knife-point, but laughter above the strain,
chucked out into the harsh world and understanding of
those who care, law and order, of homes and hostels, into
a world of tight-grip. About to be discharged, grinning,
eating on one's own. Black commander woollen beret,
playing James Blunt on Walkman, a new start and a new
beginning.

120. Hour-Glass

Yellow ochre sand 60 minuets or the 24th part of the day,
an hours journey.
A loose watery sand, to proceed with difficulty, biting
eyes, stinging cheeks,
Smudged tears, sifted through my fingertips and
hurricane winds
Blew it into the ocean.

.

121. Turn

'I love you,' he said, as he turned into dust, eyes like
coals glowing in the dark.
Under the sand in places cut off by the tide.
Jagged teeth of the sea, munching pebbles,
seaweed swims.
A tide of maximum amplitude after new and full moon
When the forces of the sun and moon act in the
same direction
An outcry calling upon all to pursue.
Someone who is to be made prisoner.
To clasp close with the arms, to embrace, to cherish.
The sea weaves its hair, cold, hidden by clouds.
From the core of the Earth.
Will he come back with the tide.

122. Breeze'less

Gentle breezes.
A whispered rumour.
To give off or reflect light.
To beam with steady radiance, to glow.
To keep one's position quietly and unobtrusively,
Where sitting together never ends.
In the midst of the heartbreak acid lines the tongue.
Thinking of warmer summer days.

123. A Shout

So thin, lean, hollow-eyed and gaunt
from weariness, hunger.
Creepy with the waves, in shadow, as your eyes
met mine.
To set the teeth together and withdraw the lips in pain,
You wiped away the dribble, and sniffed,
Lost, forlorn, and then you smiled,
And the seawater twinkled and sparkled in a haze
of bright sunshine.

124. Splash

The waves, the winds and the tides,
Shall wash us away together,
Knotted with seaweed under a full moon,
Laughing forever, foreheads touching,
Shiver.

Part Three - Love Doesn't Make Any Sense

125. Come To The Church

The church is for you
the church is for me
if you are blind
if you can't see
then come to the church.
Rather we see
and the church is for you
and the church is for me.

A Song

126. Be

No hope in a star, no hope travelling far
No hope in a star, no hope to bee hee
No hope in a star, no hope travelling far
No hope in a star, no hope to bee hee
No hope in a star, no hope to be far,
No hope in a star, no hope to bee hee
No hope to bee, he he he he
No hope to bee, he he he he
And when time runs out
And when time runs out
And when time runs out
No hope to bee hee
And when time runs out
And when time runs out
And when time runs out
No hope to bee, he he he he he he
No hope to bee, hee hee hee hee
Hee hee hee hee
No hope to bee
No hope to bee
Hee hee hee hee
No hope to bee
Hee hee hee hee
No hope to bee
Hee hee hee hee
No hope to bee
Hee hee hee hee

Be Cont'd

No hope to bee
Hee hee bee hee
Bee bee bee bee
Bee bee bee bee
Bee bee bee bee
Bee bee bee bee
No hope, no hope, no hope, no hope,
No hope, no hope, no hope, no hope,
No hope, no hope, no hope, no hope,
No hope, no hope, no hope, no hope,
No hope, no hope, no hope, no hope,
No hope to bee be be
Be ah be ah be ah be ah be
Ah be ah be ah be ah be
Ah be ah be ah bee
No hope to be, ah be ah be, ah be
Ah be, ah be, ah be
Ah be, ah be, ah be, ah be
No hope, no hope, no hope, no hope, no hope,
No hope, no hope, no hope, ah be, ah be, ah be,
Ah be, ah be be ah be, ah be ah, be be be be be be
Except in you.

A Song

127. Ribbons Of Love

The pink ones for you
The blue ones for me
And weeee will be together in eternity
The pink ones for meee
The blue ones for youuu
And wee wee wee will be in eternity
The moon shining bright
The stars in the night
The glow ow ow ow ow ow ow ow ow
The rain through the tall trees
And we will not show ow ow ow over the years.

The pink ones for meee
The blue oneuuums for you
And I'll love you
And I'll love you
And I'll love you
And I'll love you
And I'll love you
And I'll love you
It shows in your eyes
The crystals shine
From your eyes to mine
And together in eternity
We combine
We combiine
We combiine
We combiine
We combiine

Ribbons Of Love Cont'd

We combine
The pink ones for meee
The blue oneuuuums for you
And together we will
Shine in eternity
The blue ones for me
The pink ones for you
And I'll love you
Rubber lips.

128. Flight

We grow day by day in each others love
Content with companionship
A friendship, a bond
Caring for one another
With a candle lit burning
Out the seconds of time.

129. Fate

We battle with
the tides as
one
a togetherness
complete
only in a time
warp
can we become
united as one.

130. Radiation

He didn't feel a thing
not even a pinprick in the
rain sobbing tears kept on
the inside a straight face
bursting with joy
until the sun came out
and fire showed in his teeth.

131. Nettle

And the sun went down
and took with it
my earth.

132. Touch

Nothingness burned into light
when I saw your face
the bluebells danced and
rang their bells
as your lips touched mine
the world sang.

.

133. Waterlogged

Tears in the rain as he fights back
the icicles

134. Bib

Flying sleep stillness
but for the beating of your heart.

135. Forever

I love you until time
runs out and I am
forever in your arms.

136. Darkness

I love you until the stars come out
of their pockets for nightfall.

137. Night

Silver lines the night sky
as your eyes sparkled in the snow.

138. Mist

Foggy tears, bloated nose, red eyes,
tired but in paradise.

139. Melted

I love you until raindrops appear on the window ledge,
your tears while we are apart.

140. Rain

Rooftop solitary, still, where have the birds gone in the rain fall.

141. Tear

Open windows cried and banged, when there was no wind because they couldn't let you in.

142. Furnace

You were a force like the sun and I could not bear to be parted.

143. Call

The wind howled and cried out your name and I couldn't hide from you any longer.

144. Spoon

Sugary, lips devouring the senses.

145. Wild

In this wilderness a weed bloomed blue and I knew you
had heard by the quiver of the cobwebs in the corner of
the brick wall.

146. Plaster on a Knee

A faulty lace blown by the wind, undone, to trip you up, a
grazed knee with grit marks, numb leg, walk with a limp
forever with a crutch to slow you down against the wind
until snowdrops poured down and I was forever in your arms.

147. Ice

I was crying out for him in the snow and all I got was a
blizzard.

148. Look

We were pelted as we passed through the snow and all
we got was mud puddles. I put my hand in the water and
saw your reflection and you looked at me and bowed
your head as if to say, 'That's enough.'

149. You

I was crying out for you in the snow and all I got was a miracle.

150. Snow

He carried my body through the snow to stop my heart
from weeping in a pool of melted ice.

151. Knees

Two ice blocks melted together in a frozen zone.

A Song

152. Don't

And they don't really say what they don't really do that
the oxygen level is meant for me and for you and they
don't really say what they don't really dooo that the
oxygen level is here for me and yoou, and they don't
really say and they don't really dooo that the oxygen
level is here for you hoo hoo and they don't really mean
what they don't really say when the oxygen level is going
awaahay and they don't really say what they don't really
dooo that the oxygen level is here for me and yoo hoo.

A Song

153. Ice Zone

By the light of the moon we'll be on our waaay, by the
light of the moon we'll be on our waaay by the light of
the moohoon we'll be here to stay, by the light of the
moooon we'll take it a wahayaaaaa, by the light of the
moon by the light of the moon, by the light of the moon,
by the light of the moon, by the light of the moon, by the
light of the moohoon, by the light of the moon, by the
light of the moohoo, by the light of the moon, by the light
of the moon, by the light of the moon, by the light of the
moon, we'll be here to staaayhay, we'll be here to
staaaayhay, we'll be here to stay, we'll be here to stay,
forever and a daaayaa, forever and a daaayaa, by the light
of the moon, by the light of the moon, entwined in ice.

154. Garden

A speck in my heart has been missing since you went
away, first one on the back of the old wooden bench on
the left where you used to sit. Then three others on the
same bench on the right side went missing. The gaps in
the back of the old rotten wood remind me of you when you
used to sit on there and I would follow you down the
corridor through to the overgrown garden where we
would sit combing thoughts in the wild fresh air.

155. Fire grate

Your love is like being at home like a birds nest, honey in spring,
dew drops on the lawn, bird prints in the snow, storms outside
a blizzard but warm, dry and hot inside resting beside the fireplace
as the coals glisten your eyes light up the fire.

156. Now

With your warm hand in mine a thousand yesterdays are forgotten
and a place in your heart takes away the frozen stare and softens
the glare into tears of happiness and contentment knowing you
are there always with your love and we hug as one through the pain
of being apart.

157. Tide

His tears washed
With salt against
The night.

158. Rain

Banging on the window,
Rain pouring out of his soul,
Waiting to be let in
Into my warm arms.

159. Nest

I love you, you are so content with your silver beard as in sunshine
of ginger, brown and silver like snow and warm in winter.

160. Solid

A statue of snow
And then your
Eyes blinked
And I knew
We were safe.

161. Front

Kissing your stiff
Icy stubble
Your eyes
Watered
Tears of
Happiness.

162. Heat

Your mouth
Was tight
Amongst tears
Of loneliness
But heat returned
As I touched
Your face
A glow in your
Eyes said it all
As we hugged
In the snow and the
Warmth of the sun
Caressed our tears
As we kissed in soft
Petals of ice.

163. Never

I could lie with you for a thousand years
And never get up except to kiss you,
Tender petals blowing in the wind
Whisper upon my cheek and say,
I love you, forever, and ever, and ever.

164. You

I could go to sleep in your arms
In a thousand yesterdays,
Forever and a day
Your lips against mine
Hugging in tenderness
Cheeks pressing strong together
Amongst the tears sprung
From a heart so rare
Together in eternity
We will always be,
At the mercy of the tide
Enveloped inside the waves
Sparkling in sea-dust.

165. The End

A younger version of the sun,
Brought the moon down,
And the stars.

166. Star-crust

I'll love you
Until the sun burns out
And the moon is split
We are as a star, in a fire-ball.

167. Sparkling

The naked sky was pink
As there was an eclipse.

168. Tent

Dew fell across the grass
And touched your legs
In a spiders web, buttercups
Tickled and spiky grass prodded
Our back as we lay numb as one
In a deep sleep as there was
No despair but only an ice-zone
Which had melted with our hot
Breath and sweat from our glands,
As we craved for the stars
With the moon shining down
We cradled in each others arms
In a stormy embrace, clutching
So no one could part us until we
Fell asleep moulded in passion
And dirty socks.

169. Lips

You put a dagger
In my heart
When you gave me
The cold shoulder
Tears ran down my
Nose in a rain-storm
I wiped my eyes
With my runny finger's,
And you put your
Forehead on mine
And whispered....

'I LOVE YOU.'

Part Four - Melted Icicles

170. Peace

He blew cobwebs, into dust and said he didn't like the dew lights
shining
and then smiled but could see crystals in my eyes and held my hands
and said, 'I love you more than anything,' he then turned violently
and he walked way into the distance with tears in his eyes
he walked back pushed me against the wall with his hands on my
cheeks he kissed me and said, 'You are beautiful and I will never
let you down,' and put his forehead on mine, 'I will never leave
you,' he looked at my feet, held my hands and we kissed, 'I love you
so much,' he said, and then walked into the distance and a street lamp
shone in the rain.

171. Goose Pimples

You are my light, my guiding
light, shiver over the sea.
the rain pours down your hair
dribbling with surf and salt
taste of the sea. We held
hands, a tight grip shivering
in paradise, hands holding,
driftwood to make a fire
and rocking to sleep in firelight
numb senses.

172. Coffee Break

Raining goose pimples on water, shimmering cold light, icy wind blows
howling through gaps in the window, blowing curtains banging
windows, shiver, icy fingers, magpie totters on grass pecking insects,
long turquoise tail, white, black, deep blue plumage, pointed beak, the
colour of coal, tapping overgrown grass, fingers taste the cold on painted
window ledge as magpie sprints away. Hot coffee is served, thick milk
skimmed, poured hot from metal pot, stirred to ferment, dripping on the
floor to mouth chocolate biscuits in canister, the wind blows and the sea
is glistening.
    Sunlight in a rainstorm, magpie fly on grey tiles and look down
soaring high and away. Overgrown flowers hang in their baskets as we
drink our tea and meditate our thoughts long forgotten in time to be
remembered. Dainty crow flapping to the chorus of the wind. A twig
waves to the beat of the air in rhythm to the draught. Seagull croak a
hoarse loud shrill sound, snowy body fly past with their large wings and
windows blow open, skim the ocean as an empty cigarette packet is
flung across the grass.

173. Absence

The blunt edge of nothingness wasted away. Petals in the
snow turned into ice powdered silk split onto concrete
stone and rainbow colours appeared causing laser beam
shadows which danced in the moonlight until the setting
of the pink sun.

174. Morning

Stinging tears on window, wiped with a nettle, spitting in
cold puddle, dents in water like the emptiness in my
heart, terrified of scaring away the only love I ever had
which has dissolved into grey concrete and splattered puddles.

175. Look

Weeds growing on rooftops waving and drinking in the
fresh rain. How refreshing to be out in the wild with no
thoughts, but the feel of the cold wind, rain, soggy hair
and bloated eyes, with the drizzle upon my face, fighting
back the tears, rose thorns in my heart, waiting for petals
to bloom, just around the corner and out of disaster.

176. Figure

Why do you haunt me with your love and care.
Tenderness in a kiss with words from the soul, I abide in
your arms, you pull back my hair, and tell me, 'That's
better.'

177. In Heaven He Said

I love you like the birds sing,
You make me fly.

178. Words From Him

Your face is gifted and its mine
A kiss like the seashore to last for a thousand years.

179. He Said

You make me radiant
Your hair is in sunlight.

180. Fly

Our friends the seagulls to pluck up courage of grace uncertain. Come to visit us each morning having excessive self-esteem, arrogant, haughty, having a proper sense of self-respect. Flying past our window from heaven gracefully they rise, they watch and wait in the garden and answer back when you talk to them, having an appearance of pride, vigour, boldness and freedom. Stately, high-spirited, fearless, is so easily elegant in form or manner they glide over your head with their beaks held high, proud, strong, a compensating virtue or quality yet gentle like doves of peace, the undeserved mercy of God, divine influence, giving cause for pride, they nod their heads and listen. Affectedly elegant and refined manners and behaviour, attentively when you speak and watch when they go out and know where you live and where you go for walks in the forest. They come in swarms to be fed by the fish monger, living in conditions of ease, plenty, and good taste, exclamations of surprise. We love them, they love us, don't let anyone harm our wonderful friends.

181. Knelt

You sat near me and the heavens opened up
And I felt joy.

182. Content

You smiled as you left and I knew you
Felt peace and happiness.

183. Left

Your absence makes me happy
As you leave behind joy.

184. Feeling

I feel happy and content knowing your thoughts
Are my thoughts.

185. Closer

Safe, warm, feeling your
Stubble cheek in your arms.

186. One

Love in
Eternity
As one

187. Wink

You kissed me and my teardrop
You blinked into your eye.

188. Passion

You licked my snot
Over my mouth in a warm embrace.

189. Nod

As you rubbed your check against me in a tight hug
All the troubles melted and night was a thousand stars.

190. Bye

You looked knowing I was waiting for you to go and as
you went into the sunset you took my soul.

191. Flake

As crystals fall against our bodies we are covered as the flakes mould
our frozen forms. In clusters of diamonds we embrace hibernating
waiting for the spring to come when we can dance amongst the tulips
and pick blue bells, deep in the forest of make believe talking to our
friends the twig trees who dance in the moonlight, as we stand against
the wild flowers in the light of a thousand stars. The moon leaves a sigh
of relief as our love blooms against the sky enveloped in darkness of
true love.

192. Clusters

Your arms are firm and you are in control of make believe, you wipe a
tear from my eye and laugh then kiss me in torment and never ending
peace. You wipe your lips on my cheek and say you can't live without
me and I am your life, we hold each other against the wind and the sky
darkens but our love keeps us alive.

193. Time Forgotten

I will never forget this time because I know that one day
you will be gone, you say that will never be and as we stay
in each others arms you put out your finger on my lips
And say, 'forever.'

194. Spider

Blowing in the wind tear drop spider web
Cut up and dragging along the shelf
Like diamonds glistening in the wind.

195. Mist

Fine specks of frozen rain in a fountain on the window.

196. Elevensis

The air is cold and howls
Raindrops from telephone wires
And hangs as a crow flies past and croaks
In the cold morning air.

197. Present

As I give you a rose
With my love it falls
Into snowflakes,

198. Shelter

Hugging against the wind
In a safe place in the sand
With a stormy sea
Protected by rocks
And your strong arms
Wind shelter against the cold.

199. Shade

I love you
Until time runs out
And the clock casts a shadow
Looking out on the yellow horizon your eyes
Are looking out of the window many miles away
And we can see happiness together.

200. Sea Salt

Sand is in our eyes, sand on our mouths rubbing gritted cheeks.
Licking nose, rubbing foreheads, shaking seaweed hanging from
our hair. With the sound of the ocean I hear seagulls above
the waves. Our spit clean mouths and we kiss in tenderness
and blink eyes from our eye lashes brushed by the wind.
Your eyes examining in hunger and laughter, you blow a bubble
and we kiss in heated emotion with the tide in full battle.

201. Moonlight

The sea rises up and I see your face beneath the waves, you beckon
and hold my hand. We surf into unknown lands, green and blue
waves, white gushing foam, pink and orange sun. A mixture of
Purple darkens the sky. At night grey and black, the sea shimmering,
as we bathe the waves circle around our knees and we shiver
and hug shaking together. You look at me, I look at you our eyes
meet, you blink foam out of your eyes and wipe your nose with hand.
Grab me and we embrace beneath the waves.

202. Way

He said we must go in different directions, safe into his
arms, we hugged and he said, 'It was never to be,' and
then he said, 'He can't live without me,' and pushed me
away and said, 'I am with you for eternity.' I backed away
and he laughed and pushed me against the wall. The
moon came out in the final embrace, and he put his finger
on my chin and said, 'Forever,' before smouldering me
into dust. We blew into the wind.

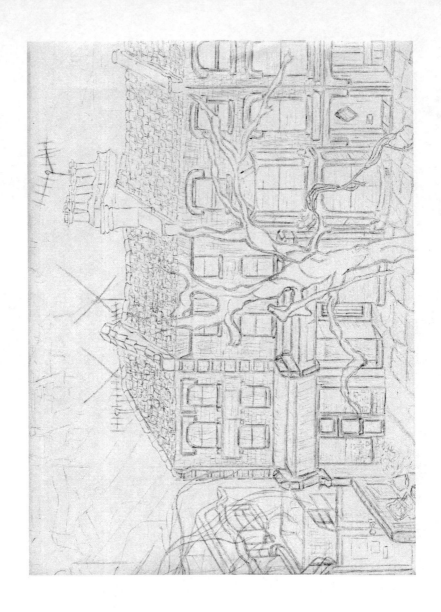